Mentha Spicata El Corazón!

Written by Jesse Cale
Cover and illustrations by Chavilah Bennett
Layout by Jason Turner

A special thanks to the moon

MENTHA SPICATA EL CORAZON!

Mentha Spicata El Corazon!
5x8 Second Edition Paperback
978-0-9984381-1-5
Published by Secret Midnight Press

www.secretmidnightpress.com

From the tippiest of toes,
down the well of my imagination,

Or like my heart is a ship
and my mind is the storm,

Follow me out the window,
rounding corners of the soul,

Finding deeper depths than darkness goes and words that only
managed to escape by hand.

This is
Mentha Spicata El Corazón!

A collection of poems, journal entries, quips, pleasantries,
retorts, and personal idioms from age sixteen to twenty six,
arranged in days and moods.

*If you are sensitive to subjects of death, suicide, depression,
and other dark/mature content,
please be wary between pages 94 and 126.
I care about you.*

Spearmint, or spear mint;

A member of the biological kingdom Plantae.
Genus: Mentha
Species: M. Spicata
Binomial name: Mentha Spicata

Spearmint is a species of mint. (also known as *Mentha Viridis*)

Viridis (Latin): adj
1. Green.
2. Young, Fresh, Lively, Youthful

Corazón;

translation from Spanish
1. Heart (anatomy)
2. Heart (emotion/feeling)
3. Sweetheart/Darling (appellative)
4. The core (fruit)
5. The center or centre (central)

Mentha Spicata El Corazón

idiom:
1. Refresh the creative heart.
2. Renew the mind.
3. Give life to the soul.
4. Desire a sense wonder.
5. Introduce something new to your life as to inspire.
6. (An artist's blessing to another artist)
   a. To wish life and inspiration upon someone.
   b. To suggest hope, reexamination, exposure to avant-garde influence.

And in his typical fashion on candle nights like this, he jumped on top of the long dining table, throwing his hands into the air; one with his fingers spread wide and the other holding an enthusiastic glass of wine.

"Mentha spicata el corazón!" he shouted. "To all of you, my sweet wonderful bags of sparkling stardust, I wish life to you. I wish nothing less than true inspiration to the deepest parts of your soul. That your minds and hearts would explore the laughter of every new thing and be wrapped in ribbons of every single sweet emotion, from the ones found in heaven to the darkest in darkness! That writer's block will be no block, but a stepping stone to something greater. I toast you and your sense of wonder, new life!"

"Mentha spicata el corazón!" someone interrupted from the back of the hall, causing a roar of cheers and whistles. A shorter woman quickly made her way to the top of the red shelf just behind me.

"Rise again to your medium with new eyes! Celebrate one another and each freckles place!" She continued. "Let any every be every any and every tool of the tongue, hand, heart and mind!" she finished, smiling much wider than before. Jesse raised his glass to her and went on.

"That every soul seeking soul's search would rest, even briefly, when encountered with your art and that the life of a moment would find meaning in your self-expression. So tonight, my friends, a toast to it all, and to it all and to you, I say mentha spicata el corazón!"

"Mentha spicata el corazón!" we loudly toasted each other in response.

This is a space

A magic little place

Where your mind can rest

And your heart can race

So turn the page
and come inside
Your secret midnight
Place to hide.

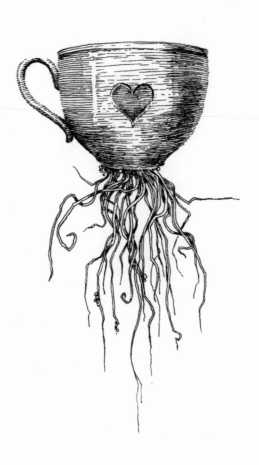

MENTHA SPICATA EL CORAZÓN!

the sun washes like old steel

i'm flying like a violin

my mind isn't at rest though

i have that obligation sensation

that pre-intrude mood

my mind's in that invade grade

"not i" said i "but they" said me

i want to taste berries and grapes

not apples

but strawberries

then raspberries

take me to the city where i'm always looking from the top of the tallest

"i've never been there" my mind sighed

"maybe someday" my eyes responded

dear world

touch your toes

then tilt back and squint your eyes

run!

breathe!

the sun's fingertips are exactly where i'd like to stand

he will wash me like old steel

"fresh out of the dirt" he will say

"i'm alive" i will think

"you're alive" you will say

i turned my head from you while i smiled

now i'm running

hello everything!

look what i've found!

(She won't remember the sky and how it would bark in
different shades. I was away when it was born.)

Hush

There's a hush in me,
like when the wind stops or the bottom of a breath.

You're lurking in the reflections of lights
and humming in the distance of darkness.

The retired acrobat of my heart hears the roar of an encore.
I feel a tumble in his footsteps, but with a pace unbridled.

His memory, antique, unfolds like a map
and I trace my way back to shivers down the spine.

You're a soft sound as my heart drums louder.

Hush.

Talk of the town

I don't want the talk of the town
I want the love of my life
Relentlessly longing for who you were
The one before the vase fell
The veil removed
Constantly reminded of the restlessness in my longing to be
nurtured
In the grass and in the night
A soft song and every hummingbird
My heart groans hollow like a whistle in the wind
Subtle sparkles in the eyes of my memory
And one hand reaching up from a dark depth to break the sur-
face of my future
Looking for a savior
Don't be my savior
Just follow me
comfort me.

Falling Asleep III
Honey III

One two three,
up the honey tree.

Swings settling slowly,
running up the window sill.

Birds flew and up it rises,
babbling brook or candy cane.

Gentle grass, sweet breeze,
fall asleep, bumble bees.

Eyes with freckles and many moons,
movement left and right.

A carriage draws a top hat
and a candle rules the night.

Spinning.

Sometimes I wonder if the places I dream about are real.

I daydream of dreaming in my dream house

CHAVILAH

I woke up in heaven at Chimney Crest

I woke up to a sunrise kissing
Sweetly on my toes,
Up my feet,
Onto my nose.

I woke again to color casting
Over rolling hills.
A cast to catch the perfect picture
When a cup of autumn spills.

I woke up to a quiet light, whispers
Motherly and calm,
Out my mouth,
Into my palm.

This home creaks with a hundred rooms,
A thousand windows more,
If I need heaven, ring the bell,
You'll find me at the door.

Scraps

scraps and scraps
up to the windows

piles on the floor
and under the couch

pieces of paper
one piece at a time

if i keep saying no
the higher they'll climb

scraps and scraps
up to the windows

piles on the floor
and under the couch

pieces of paper
one piece at a time

my mind is a mess
but it will always be mine

Hello to you
Clouds bursting in blue
My head's upside down
And the sun's shining through

A Sweet Baby

Knit together to knit

Adolescent, candle lit

Self discovery looked different
and the emotions were strong

The heart of an infant
and the soul of a fawn

Built up to build

A sweet baby, strong willed

Defining prematurely
and decisions too young

Started climbing too early
Exercising his tongue

A sweet baby came crashing
He fell to his knees

But when he stood up
He was taller than trees

The days that I remember who I am are the best days.

Every decision I've ever made
allowed me today.

Patience

Burning like a dying ember,
To be doused, to become too cold,
To burn again.
Or, the air, a sweet wind,
Like water to wild flowers,
Breath under my feet and I burn again.

But patience,
Patience is your touch once,
To wait again.
Patience is standing at the harbor,
Patience saw their children off to war
And patience buried their loved ones.
To meet again is patience.
To grow hungry is patience.

An alarming sound, far away, is patience
The same way that closing your eyes
Is patience.
The night is patience.
Your lips, in a dream, is patience.

In my palm like a smooth stone,
In my eyes, the focus,
In my ears like a song near by
And the places that I put my feet,

A decision,
Patience.

Is it a blessing (or a curse)
that apathy (or ignorance)
has kept me from giving up (or giving in)

apathy

I feel no shiver
There's no sound to my shake
Not dead
But lifeless
Not empty
But nothing at all
Color, not even a memory
Sound, no tune to touch me
Not joy misplaced, but no place for it

Quiet with
not a thought to vacate

Half-hearted would imply a heart to call,
but my descriptions virgin
or my chest is barren
Nihility is the dogma of my spirit
The lacuna of my life

This is
not
a nightmare
nor
a daydream
but waking nothing to life as I'm awake to nothingness

I'm always
out the window

Black and White

"*no more colors*" my eyes said

"*no more beautiful colors*" my mind regrets

my peach skin gives off light grey

my blue eyes give off dark grey

my dirty feet leave black prints

and my mind is covered in spots

Happiness

When I close my eyes and think of happiness, I hear a piano
Just a few notes
                              Major
                                        Here and there
A sunrise even   Off in the distance
                    Above the trees
                                        Subtle earth tones
Lowly saturated blues and
Cool water from a stream up to my ankles
The sweet sound of birds
A clean hand brushes against mine when I think of happiness

I go there in my daydreams
                              The only thing left behind is my body

I've spent my life trying to separate romantic melancholy from
happiness

                              But there's something about the Fall
That is like the clean hand brushing against mine when I think
                                        of happiness

Someday I'll wake up and my body will be there with my day
dreaming mind

                                        For the first time

I WANT TO KISS
THE AUTUMN COLORS.

What if Autumn

Fantastic Fall fantasies filling my already full mind.
The burnt reds, yellows, and browns are licking my toes
and painting each step.

I want to wake up with my wife's fingers in my mouth
and then pour eachother tea, because that's the only way to
have real luck.

The water will be fresh and babble like a brook when it's time
to steep.
The gray backdrop will be a perfect fit to the mild depression
that matches one minor to three major piano chords.

This is all just a fantasy as I find myself
perfectly birthed into a home of what ifs.

Hello to you
You're so very sweet
I can't help but smile
Each time we meet

Summer, my lady

Summer slips into a hand woven dress
and slippers of sweet strawberry tints by the light of a dirty
window.

She moves the air like the spins of a carousel
as she acts a puppeteer of romance, tying stomach knots with
my heart strings.

She's whispering while winter waits one moment longer,
just enough time to count the stars.

I'm beige to her curtsy, but red to a memory.
I blush of dying colors.

I'm sad to see her go —
Summer, my lady.

You don't have to be happy, but being happy sure is nice.

You don't have to be happy, but being happy sure is nice

You don't have to be happy, but being happy sure is nice.

You don't have to be happy, but being happy sure is nice

You don't have to be happy, but being happy sure is nice

you don't have to be happy, but being happy sure is nice.

YOU DON'T HAVE TO BE HAPPY

you don't have to be happy, but being happy sure is nice.

you don't have to be happy, but being happy sure is nice.

you don't have to be happy, but being happy sure is nice.

you don't have to be happy, but being happy sure is nice.

You don't have to be happy, but being happy sure is nice.

You don't have to be happy, but being happy sure is nice.

The drawstring to shut eye

A hard day's work
Your best

Sleep well
Good rest

Lay low
Lazy day

Restless soul
Fade away

Falling Asleep IV

My legs submit
And my eyelids wave.
My breath lands close to me
And my arms don't try.

My mind dips and slips and swims
Through half heart half-thoughts
As my tongue dances with my teeth off-duty.

There's a star in the distance,
Small sweet light.
I'm just leaving my body
Just for the night.

Though if dreams took up residence
I'd wish for much longer.
The reality is
In dreams I'm much stronger.

where do you go when
You can't sleep?

I go where MY
imagination
takes Me.

MY IMAGINATION IS AS FAR AS
I GO
IN SOME CASES

IN OTHERS

IT'S JUST THE BEGINNING.

I have magical powers
when I don't sleep.

I can't even say I have late nights anymore.
They've all become mornings.

Five

It's nearly 5 in the morning.
There's no sign of twilight yet.
The sun is still under the covers kissing with the clouds
and the moon has had a hard time dealing with her distant
relatives.

They send their regards in tiny pieces.

I can't wait to see the face of the sun.
That sun will surely be wearing a different expression com-
pared to the face he posed so vividly.

Will he finally speak today,
or will he hold his tongue
much like the wise man that he is?

The shades are smiling
Waking up

The shades are smiling again.
They tease me each morning.

They were in a different mood just hours ago, I swear it.

I reach and pull
and they sing their song,

A squeaky voice that I've grown to love.

A sigh of relief from both them and I.
The sun is here and it's right in my eyes.

The sun is a cool beam!

Sweet in color
And I'm always raising my hands

And through my fingers
My toes will tingle like sugar, but feel like sand

Take me in and let me be with you
For all time, I'm ready

The greater side of my mind consumes the rot when I feel your
love

So please, open
your doors
The ones I believe you have
Accept me
take me
in

My bed
My boat

Sea is calm.
The sound of rain makes my hair stand,
like a cold breath of a lover to the back of my neck.
The sky is a reflection of a down comforter.

My hearts humming another song today,
In my little wooden boat
Reclined
like a flower in the rain.

I feel no pressure to row,
To kick my legs eagerly
in the wake,
like a bird
aimlessly
flapping,
There's nowhere to go but here
and here I am.

A Persian rug lines my bones and jewels garnish my face.
A prince where I am,
A prince where I go,
The king is my father
as I rest in my boat.

The grass isn't greener, in fact, it's just fine right here.

Dear Jesse

It's been weeks now since you've seen anything in color. It feels the same as seeing nothing at all. I'm sorry that you're in another season of hollow sorrow and deep sadness; It's truly heart breaking. You've always had a heart full of romance, boy. The things you do really make people proud. You're a living example of hope to lots of people even though it isn't always how you feel. It's a challenge keeping that silly head up, but I know you prefer the stars over the dirt.

Love,
Jesse

And forever more!

And forever more!
And forever more!
And has always been!
It is love that drives me.

It is not food that shakes my bones to life,
It is not water dripping from my fingertips,
It is love! Pulling me up from my bed.

Take my bread, crush my home,
Just leave my love,
my lover,
my sweet humble song
that I sing so loudly through the streets in the day
and hum in the candles to the light cast upon her.
It's love!

It's words and it's teeth,
My teeth
to her bones,
My tongue
to her heart,
Her words
to my eyes, oh they swell with love,
always swelling with love.

Oh the break in my soul,
It's broken, but I still see love.

It's a bright day
hidden inside shattered pottery,
Smashed by my love,
But recovered by
love.

I'm kissing you
in my mind
And I'm kissing you
in my mind still.
Come closer,
The swell of my eyes bursts
every moment
for you.

I'm living to love till death
where love will be with me, will complete me,
as always completed by love.

Oh God, give me this love,
The dark in me has died because of love, and with no love,
I am nothing to myself

and nothing to my love.

ONE DAY
I WILL FALL
INTO THE SEA

I WILL STAY THERE

I WILL BE THE ANCHOR
FOR YOU.

When you're cute

Cute is a bouncing piece of the sun
As cute as a button
As cute as a bird

Cute is a berry held tight in your palm
As cute as a wiggle
As cute as a noise

When your mouth curls up like a ribbon of pink
As cute as the morning
As sweet as a breeze

And from the moment I see you
Till the moment I sleep
As cute as the picture
Of you that I keep

Holiday lights

Holiday lights
through wet eyes,
Exploding crystals
as your back bends —
beautiful architecture.
My stronghold that
I want to decorate
every moment with a
cherry flake blood
rush to your toes and
with a kiss.
Your eyes,
pools of
love for me,
selfishly dilate
when the fireworks
would come —
a time of celebration.
Like a sky
exposed of shooting stars,
sporadic nail marks
connect freckles.

No more
innocence
when you
conquered me,
above me,

you made me
your resting place —
a knot
impossibly
made.

The house would
burn down
around us
every time
I found you
in my room.

Each second
was a secret
we wanted
Everyone
to know,
because
creation
is as
great as
passion is
loud!

Hello to you
My heart is missing
It's run off with yours
Hugging, kissing

Cuddle you, baby

My left arm laid long to my side
and her heart was the perfect shape.

She fit so well nestled touching noses,
Cheek flushed roses,
Lips touched lingering,
And hair curls fingering.

Fools become wise men once the foolishness has gone,
And I've become a dreamer with the love I'm resting on.

Twist me daisies
Honey II
Falling Asleep II

I'm having wine.

Deep down the wishing well and purple ponds of lush floating
green plush greens.

See you in the sunlight,
my love in the moonlight.

Last late nights love lights gone dim with dark red velvet
glasses.
Hands to hold, subtle passes.

Laying in a riverbed, silent,
Laying honey tasting starlight.

Sweet subtle sweet things.

Up in the branches are silhouettes of righted wrongs and you.

Climbing down to lay beside the burlap baby dreaming day
dreams at night.

Sleep tight.

Spark

I remember where I was,
Where I had been,
When I knew,
then,
still now,
that in the middle of the night
we had to flee from our home made just for loving
and just for a short while, supporting.

Children on separate knees —
One east,
One west.

It's hard to imagine that there's a spark,
I'm drawn so dearly to,
in the same world I so eagerly conquer
like a child on a hill.
You there, are there, and I must turn my head
until the spark,
The spark,
Oh the spark,
Till it's not a spark,
but good memory,
by the grace of God
a good memory.

I remember where I was,
Where I had been,

When I knew,
then,
still now,
that you only knew me where your feet touched.
That when the earth shook below
you only saw it in the waving trees
and not in me.
I was the one that shook free the apples for you to delight in.
I was the one who rung the bells
and brought the night.

Where your feet touched,
no deeper.

And if I am wrong,
then like a horse no good, broken, close my eyes.
Don't let me explore anymore shallow depths.
Like a coin for luck
to the bottom of a well,
Pilots with no hope should think of one like you.
But this one,
Let it be quick to the sea,
a race to the bottom,
Oh that beautiful deep blue.
If I am wrong,
then surely
I'll meet you there.

Forever,
My dear,
The spark.

I miss the space of laughter between
your cheeks

I miss you there
Beside me
Under the tree or
As far west till the sea
Apples and kissing
Champagne
We held hands through the grass so many times
From the sunrise of our twenties we'd wash away the past
Kissing again and again

I MISS YOU THERE

YOU WERE BESIDE ME

LIKE THE MOON SITS NEAR A STAR

BUMBLE BEES NEAR A FLOWER

A VOICE YOU CAN HEAR
YOU WERE THERE

The fire left burning
Is doused when I see us together
And I smile again
From you

Now from you
I miss you there
Beside me

To break your heart once
Is to break Mine twice

56 19 3 7 21 18 44

it's time to let this all be

21   3   44   19   56   7   18
figure trying out   done   im   to   things

To burn

Every time I see her,
Whether in my mind
or the word of a friend,
A voice or a sight,
Whether memory
or lost futures,

My throat burns
like a house
on fire.
My stomach
has been poisoned
and my heart
is fragile,
Teetering,
A tight rope.

The throb in my belly,
Pregnant with a raging ocean and poor colors.
The sight of a storm from a window
is my mind
and a beaten boxer
is my conscience.

I have disappointed eyes
and an upset spine.
She made a fool of a good man,
Like the wind to a nest,
She made a snake of herself.

Who is this stranger?
Surely one I've never met.

She burns the ground
And kills the trees —
She's a fire.

And I'm still burning.

I'VE BEEN ~~LIVING~~ BLINDFOLDED
SMILING
AND
WALKING
        BACKWARDS

BLINDFOLDED
SMILING
AND
WALKING
        BACKWARDS

BLINDFOLDED
SMILING
AND
WALKING
        BACKWARDS

BLINDFOLDED
SMILING
AND
WALKING
        BACKWARDS

BLINDFOLDED
SMILING

The Ghost

Oh, the ghost
The ghost
The ghost in me

Reaching out through my arms
Down through my legs
Lust in my shallows
The pain in my still

Silence my charms
Cancer for eggs
No ear for the hallows
A crack in my will

Oh, the ghost
The ghost
The ghost in me

what I thought was provision has left me
with scars.

I thought I knew what I wanted.

It's so easy to get hurt.

...AND SO KILLED IS MY LOVE FOR LOVE.

usually not to be bothered, but this time the door opens. I'm ~~~~~~ ~~~~ different about today that he should not only have his ~~~~~~, ~~~~ windows as well. My hands were numb ~~ I quickly made myself familiar by the fireplace.

"I can't seem to make sense of it," he said. "What's got you ~~~~~ to me?"

I ~~~ caught off guard, but not ~~ ~~~~~ to finally tell him the news from the Bastion ~~ ~ thinkable.

"We've been floating for nearly seventeen days."

"And you aren't dead..."

"I think it might have to do with your air," was the last thing I manage to say before the pain came ~~~

I woke up ~~ ~~~ pink and light-gray land ~~~~ ~~ ~~~~ ~~~~~~~~ during the Bastion ~~~~~~ lobby ~~~~~~~~~~ I pulled to Coralev Rouge.

"It's been sixteen days," ~~~~~~~~~~ nervously. "It's just like ~~~~~~ out the air. There's something different this time.

~~~~~~ ~~~~ chatter and smell cooking coming from the dull pink glow ~~~~~~~~~~~~~~~ serve as backdrop for ~~~~ in real life ~~~~ when ~~~~~~~~ thawing.

"They ~~~~~~~~~~~~~~~~~~~~," ~~~~~~~~~~ said.

"If you ~~~~~~~~~~~~~~~~~~~~~~~~~ I'm

the sky is no bigger than my heart

from my heart to yours is worlds apart.

From a distance
Or a ship in a bottle

The fumes of long goodbyes still linger in the rooms I've
locked shut.

A bell rings in the distance and
through rainy windows
I still see you
there,
Were always there.

The temper swelled into a thick smoke that I choked on for
months.

The breeze played on;
Someone will soon
knock to
the rhythm of
my door.

Sweet daisies will bloom in my house,
Sweet Roses
and carnations.

No sickness in the air from a foul misfortune.

We —
Spoiled,
Skewed,
Tortured.
I'm sorry forever.
A piece of me went to see you never return.

I pray it never shows up —
No face,
No sign.

Just lessons
And decisions.

Pulling on my cheeks

pulling on my cheeks
and bringing me down

just a simple sadness
and a subtle frown

still pulling up the anchor
that's tied to my heart

and picking up the pieces
from when love fell apart

Struck down

struck down, struck down
each blow to my jaw

spilled flowers and kisses
that I try to recover

struck down, struck down
each blow to my jaw

by the one who they're for
for you, my lover

Every day is a stone

Life,
One day at a time,
It's a line of smooth stones.

The first laid by the child
And the last by the old man.

Today I place my stone and the sun moves along.

When the birds sing I place a stone again.

I go
Through shipwrecks of my heart
Through sugar on my tongue
Sweet angels lullabies and true love
Crying at the sound of your name
Laughing in hysteria at the idea of the crime you committed
against me
Betrayed by my partner
Put to death by my guardian
Poisoned —

is just a stone.

And today,
A new stone.

Round, smooth,
Another stone.

Falling Asleep V

My teeth are soupy and gummy,
Loose like a flag stuck in mud.
My mind is an old water balloon on a picnic table.
I've got rust in my joints and a kitchen for a nose.

My moses is still a baby.

We found our way back to heaven.
No one had been there for a long time.
I went home at night and slept again,
but this time, when the sun came up, it felt plain.

I never spoke again, because heaven was empty
and so was I.

Hello to you
Your heart's a balloon
It's floating away
Up to the moon

I WANT TO
FLOAT AWAY

If you feel like you're floating away
just remember
You'll be closer to the stars

Close your eyes and smile

Oh Hello!
I see you there
You're like
a little moon
A wonderful sweet sparkly thing
Be yourself
always
It's a nice thing to do

Big Baby
Waking Up II

A little quiet light of pink.
Your air in harmonies over harmonies
Again and again.
The crying stops or the crying starts.
A subtle sweet sweeping hand
Something stops still in a silence
Bigger than yourself,
But smaller than your heart.

Sing like a flower being bent to the rain
Buzz like the warmth of a heart by a fire.
See you in seated windows
Silhouetted in my dreams.

My morning home —
First thoughts half thought, once loved,
And never lived.

There's a tickle in my sunshine

There's a tickle in my sunshine
and a ripple in my rhythm.
There's a silence in my moments
and a dance in my speech.

My ears ring the way the sun shines in the morning.
My heart squeezes like lemons to my taste.

If I were to call it butterflies
I'd also call it simple;
But simple is my laughter
and deep is my vision.

There's a burn in my belly
and wings in my toes.
There's a song in my fortune
And a youth to my pose.

I want someone to make everything sweet
Someone who speaks with sugar on their tongue...

Pink, light, and brown

You twinkle and you're sweet
Like a honey jar sunset.
Your words are a nice thing,
Dropping sugar in my tea.

You're music in the next room,
My new favorite tune
Tickling taught tines in my heart.
You're a toy chest in the attic
With laughter and memories,
Fingerprints and history.

You're running out the summer screen door
Chasing fireworks to oblivion.
You'll burst yourself
Someday,
I'm sure of it!

You're falling into leaves
Constantly
Deep in my mind,
Like a breaking wave of earth tones.

I want to say you're everything,
Sometimes even anything.
But you're not, just you,
And you twinkle and you're sweet.

I want someone to

tell me it's time to start

over

That I'm a child again.

I'll tell myself that things will be ok.

I used to sleep on my dogs
I miss being little and light
The world was so much bigger
and things seemed so much heavier

...but now it is my heart that is heavy
my problems that are big

...and nothing carries much weight to my soul

just someone

not just someone to watch me hurt

...but someone to help

maybe it's just too dark and they don't know where to reach to save me.

Cast no shadow

and if that day comes
to pull the rib from me
then cast no shadow on me
lay nothing before me

to bury my sweet lover
from here, this stanza of my twenties,
will mean two things, to my right, to my left.

It will mean I found love
Under a sweet cherry blossom, she was there
Like every hour came all at once
The birds went silent as if I had stolen all the air when I gasped
I froze
Every part of me was ice
Melting to join the pools where I bathe of her eyes.

Her voice, a quiet melody that a mother sings
To my soul, to my deepest drowned rock
I would surely die if she were to touch my shoulder
To touch my mouth I would have never been born.

In a single moment I longed for her, for her, I was made for her
I was sung to life for her
I woke up today for her
I woke up the day before for her
I will wake up tomorrow for her.

She was every beautiful memory cast to the side with one
move of her hand
Her dress fit her like the last stroke to a masterpiece
And she, like a story written just to be told again
And again,
Was drinking tea.

Every monument shook with fear
Even Shakespeare spoke no more
The tongue no longer taste
The clouds hid leaving the sky exposed, embarrassed.
It was all because of her, her beauty,
And what I want to know, her heart.

She came to me
and I was all of this I was to her.

but if the day comes
to pull the rib from me
then cast no shadow on me
lay nothing before me

to bury my sweet lover
from here, this stanza of my twenties,
will mean one other thing.

It will mean the crow is my keeper
Not even a dancing leg will find me to a familiar tune, never
again
My ears are silent to every song with no remorse.
At sea in the storm, I have only contempt for the lighthouse
And like blue windows on a rainy day, any sign of life is pale
and cold.

It will mean that I've yet to leave this side of the grave,
But nor have I lived a moment longer, as if I've become a
portrait lacking all color.

The wood is rotten in me, the birds make their nest some-
where once familiar
Saplings have sprung in the dusty kitchen of my memory
The stairway of my dreams will lead you nowhere
The door has broken, the thieves are ruthless.

I'm no longer swimming in that pool, the one I once melted to join.
My sweat is no longer for passion, but for nothing at all.
The stars were never there and the light of a firework never reaches me.
My toes rest in the oil of unused emotions.

and if that day comes
to pull the rib from me
then cast no shadow on me
lay nothing before me.

The moon has been kidnapped

I trip and I tumble
Down into the darkness,
Dirt, roots, and shadows
Death, fear, and wounds.

The moon has been kidnapped
And the stars have been stolen,
The sky has gone missing
And the air is estranged.

Silence rings in my ears
Like the sound of a cellar
And my stomach is ancient,
hollow, unfed.

Muscle and bone
That my mind has forgotten,
Black is my heart
And my soul is now rotten.

THE MOON HAS BEEN KIDNAPPED

AND THE STARS HAVE BEEN STOLEN

THE SKY HAS GONE MISSING

AND THE AIR IS ESTRANGED

MUSCLE AND BONE

THAT MY MIND HAS FORGOTTEN

BLACK IS MY HEART

AND MY SOUL IS NOW ROTTEN

Pleading myself to pieces

Deep sea, swimming in my brain
Of all the things I feel,
It's pain.

I feel it the most
I see it in my shadow and hear it in my breath,
Death.

Closer than my skin to the bone
Expelling my joy in a moment
With a lifetime of dead deeds undone down wells of the dark-
est depths.

Come creeping, come slowly,
In my ears and down my spine
Shaking me from heaven to my toes.

If there is no God
I'll regret never having killed myself
As fearing him left me barren.

MY HORROR,
THIS HORROR,
OH HORROR,
DEEP DARKNESS,
THE WELL OF NO MOONLIGHT,
WHAT SUNSHINE
HAS EVER SHONE
IN THE MUCK OF
MY BROKEN HEART?

What spirit is here
and how do I leave it behind?

It fell on me like an oil soaked blanket, the darkness.
Now I revel in the blood of my fading dreams.

A sick cynic cycling circles of the drain,
Masturbating to the laughter of a foul nightmare.

The Saddest Song

A song sung sweetly
A hum under breath

A nose on his cheek bone
The quiet song of death

The lights were off
and his bed was cold

No one was there
when he died sad and old

As the song played
he felt someone near by

He said "is it death?"
Death said "it is I."

So he closed his eyes
and he sang along

To a song sung sweetly
The saddest song

I'd rather

I'd rather be talking
Or writing
Or playing dress up.

I'd rather be singing
Or laughing
Or even crying.

I'd rather be lying
Or praying
Or bending over.

But here I am in pieces
Being broken
Being eaten.

The art of the old

I've locked lips with my depression,
cheek to cheek with my death.
I've touched the hair of my sadness
and traced the heart of my sick.

I've spun a dizzy day dream,
My nightmare of a web.
I've stumbled into darkness
Rounding corners in my mind.

My fingers lace together
As I dive, or do I sink?
Am I breathing in my poison
or is it that from which I drink?

Lost inside a romance,
Imagination from a noose.
Hang, swing, till art is dead
Or till joy cuts me loose.

I FEEL LIKE EVERY PART
OF ME IS LOOKING
FOR SOMETHING.

FOR SOMETHING.
OF ME IS LOOKING
I FEEL LIKE EVERY PART

I feel like I'm falling

apart

trying

to

get

myself

together.

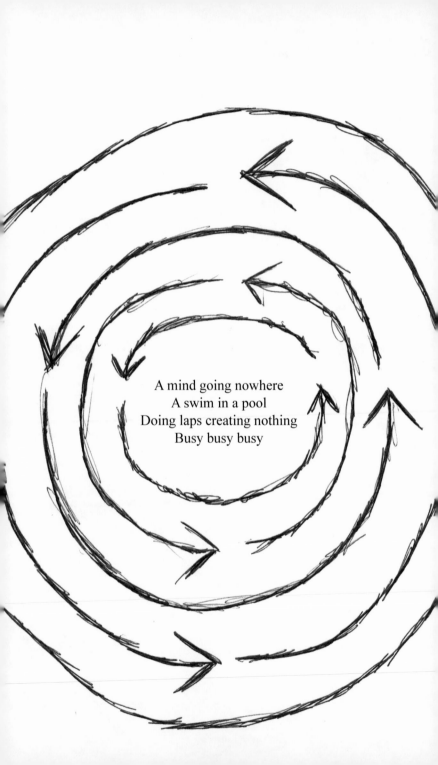

A mind going nowhere
A swim in a pool
Doing laps creating nothing
Busy busy busy

To be happy is unnatural

With a mind like mine

Every thought is a puzzle

Intuition is my master

Emotions are my gatekeeper

And darkness constantly finds me

Outside my mind, inside the present
The only place that doesn't hurt.

...So I guess I'll live in it.

You don't see what's tickling in my ears
The swimming ribbons being tugged
By a current of emotion
Tied to each end of my mind
Which infinitely feels finite
And to be felt for eternity

Harvest, Heritage

As heavy as stone
Hard, fashioned of leather

but
Brittle and small
Locked in step

Ghastly in his youth

A heritage of cold caves in lost mountains

The last thing he remembered:

That he had been, quietly, and was to be no more.

Secret Secret, The Skeleton Key

No self-control
Can't lock the doors

Two months at a time
For the grand reveal

Do you love me?
Yes.

But no,
Maybe soon.

Kill my body to save my body
Or kill my body to save my sanity

Death,
Death,

But life.

A thump and a bump

A thump and a bump
Tumbling down

It's me, he said
He heard, he saw

I'm crashing, waving
Teetering tot

Tossing and turning
A head unthought

Mumbling, grumbling
Tongue in a knot

Heaving, rowing
A life in the pot

My flesh mourned my soul
Rubbing my nose while it cried
Seeing the light in its creation
It groaned, it sighed

MY GREATEST WAR
IS THE ONE I WAGE
AGAINST MYSELF.

HOW W
FIGHT

HOW will
fight

HOW WILL I EVER
FIGHT ANYTHING ELSE?

How will I ever fight anything else?
How will I ever fight anythin
How will i ever fight anything else?

OW WILL I

FIGHT ANYTHING ELSE?

HOW WILL I FIGHT

ANYTHING ELSE?

HOW WILL I EVER
fight anything

HOW WILL I EVER FIGHT ANYTHING ELSE?

HOW WILL I EVER FIGHT ANYTHING ELSE?

HOW WILL I EVER FIGHT

EVER
THING ELSE? ANYTHING ELSE?

HOW WILL I EVER FIGHT

ever ANYTHING ELSE?

ything else?

HOW WILL I
EVER FIGHT
ANYTHING ELSE?

HOW WILL I

WILL I

How will I ever fight anything else?

How will I ever fight anything else

How will I ever fight anything else?

How will I ever fight anything else?

How will I ever fight anything else?

How will I ever fight anything else

lse? How will I ever fight anything el

How will I ever fight anything

will I ever fight anything

IT JUST TAKES
SO MUCH
SOMETIMES.
IT JUST TAKES
SO MUCH
SOMETIMES.
IT JUST TAKES
SO MUCH
SOMETIMES.
IT JUST TAKES
SO MUCH

Smile through gun smoke

Glass clouds are my eyes,
but still blue like the day,
and the day I was born.
They are heavy,
and heavy with rain.

My eyes
are not foggy,
that is
my mind,
Like the smoke of a war —
the North
and South.
A quarrel within
the boundaries of
my body, but
not confined from
my spirit
my ruby soul
my shining soul
so hurt.

The North
as my mind
The South
as my heart.
Their hands do not meet,
Nor tomorrow.

Though I'm praying
that neither suffer
great casualties,
for it is
my future, and road
possibly predestined,
taking
every bullet
and binding
every wound.

But if one should win the other,
if predestined,
I'll be scouring the fog,
the smoke,
amongst the lost,
for my smile.

It was a gift
meant to be shared,
not lost
in gun smoke.

They say you're who you really are when you're alone.

Then I guess right now I'm really me.

As dark as a man's soul is a curtain drawn against the sun.

Glory, my death

My brothers heart
My mothers eyes
These things I miss
I miss all the time.

My father's word
My lover's hand
These things I miss
I miss all the time.

Safety found
Somewhere nigh
A hundred men
For whom I'd die.

For where I grew
I grew up well
Now as a man
I'm damned to hell.

So come and take me
Bind my hands
Down the hill
Through barren lands.

Into the valley
Let me fall
To lose my shackles
I'd lose it all.

Don't watch, my lover
Don't shed a tear
Just know I'm free
As are you, my dear.

You're free from me
And all my ways
You were the light
Of darker days.

The land was sacred
As birth was pure
But life is something
I can't endure.

But glory shines
And angels sing
I'm praying peace
Is what death will bring.

And if it does
A joyous day
Because all my tears
Will fade away.

it is…

pain that travels faster than light

this is all what i saw

i lifted my head after biting the wires and i was on the side of a
dirty country road

everything was the right color

and i was looking at myself raise my head

i was surrounded by corn

here I am

surrounded by lines of corn

it's beautiful

If you're awake...

LATE INTO THE NIGHT
FEELING DARK
AND ALL ALONE

REMEMBER

THAT'S WHERE THE MOON
AND STARS ARE AT HOME.

Hope

Amidst the darkness
silence may be undone

For even at night
there's a song to be sung

For even at night
there's a poem on your tongue

Because amidst the darkness
there's a war to be won

Hope once more!

With the darkness
comes a terrible weight

When the darkness comes
Rise! create!

Pick up your brush
pick up your pen

And never be crushed
by the darkness again.

Hope is Free

free to share, free to have, free to give
free to spread, free to enjoy,
free to embrace, free to dwell on
free to feel, free to protect,
free to inspire, free to create

Hope is free, Hope is free, Hope is free
Hope is free, Hope is free...

MENTHA
EL SPICATA
CORAZON!

I must catch my train!

I must catch my train!
Every thought bursts into white.
There's no where to look
Because there's nothing to see.
I must catch my train!

A moment, one,
This time it is mine.
I've not been waiting,
There's no time to be waiting.
I must catch my train!

Words aren't even to be saved
And only as much as I can carry
Through the street,
Over the fence,
I must catch my train!

Strike a major chord!
Let it ring out!
No noose will take me to the bridge
Because I must,
I must catch my train!

Onward!
Forward!
Nowhere to look
Nothing to see

No words
Not yet
Not a chance
No, Nothing
Overwhelmed with joy.
You, come with me!
Chase what I'm chasing!

I must catch my train!

Here I come

Taps in the hall,
Feet on the floor,
Running from a life of walking on eggs.

Taps in the hall,
Feet on the floor,
Running from a life of binding my legs.

Taps in the hall,
Feet on the floor,
The past in the distance as I head for the door.

Taps in the hall,
Feet on the floor,
I'm nearly there, a slave no more.

i want to be on the other side
of the window

find me
in the sunray

i want to feel the way they told me it would feel
the way they showed me it would feel

it's not for the world
but for every soul still sleeping

wake up!
find me in the sunray

cover me in color
cover yourself in color

find me on the other side
of the window

i'll be there waiting
wrapped in yarn

no more secrets
it's written on my face

Imagined I'm a bird
and remembered once more

That all it took was faith
to jump, to soar

What's stopping you?

When you can't keep it together
It's best to share your heart
A safe place for the pieces
If you start to fall apart.

Sparkle

Bat, Flash, Flicker
Flutter, Glimmer, Glitter
Beam, Burst, Glow
Sparkle, Shine, Explode!

Do what you love

and love what you do

and always sleep well

The rugs of Gods

Drift away if you're tired,
Under bohemian woodgrain,
By the spices of romance,
with a fragrance like coffee.

Lay on rugs and giggle,
Like your belly's a miracle
And your eyes are your mouth.

If you're sad be a baby,
Be a crashing wave too.
I've got bags of magic to shake in you!

So go to sleep in a sunbeam,
Go to hell in car,
See heaven through glasses,
And shit in the stars.

Falling Asleep I

Sing the song of the rain
Midwest sweet sap
Maple syrup
Honey bee

Rub my tongue with your ginger
Touch my toes with your clovers
Feed my eyes with your lion's mane
Cross my heart with your roses

Climb up my temple
And reach in to my mouth
Find what I'm mumbling
And jump off the mountain
Take my wings to my sternum
And float to my belly

I'm a wax made of spring
And a clay from the stone
While the hands of an oak tree
Come brushing the wind

Questions in rhyme schemes
And lessons in whistles
Whales gone swimming
And boats gone missing

Old soap lathered
An old window cill
Leaves in the wind
Finger tips touching water
Butterflies while you wait

My eyes
are closing
Slowly

I'm being rushed

to my rest

Lips

aren't responding

No need

Sweet dreams

Go to sleep with a good attitude

If you're feeling restless
If you're feeling dark
Gather a notebook and pencil
Draw circles, make art

Or
Write a story, start small

If that doesn't do it
Go make some tea

And if you're too impatient
Go stand on your head
Stand till you fall
Propped up on the wall

And if that doesn't work
Put on a song
Lay there
Just listen

If that isn't it

Don't write
Don't call
I've done what I can
And it did nothing at all.

STAY SPARKLY,

MOONBEAM

I feel nearly there
Everything is beautiful

But I'm just an observer

I want to be part
Of the beauty

And be kissed
On the cheek

I want to trust
And believe
The love

take a step towards me

it's a hello

and i'm always grateful

just got off the phone with the sun!
  He can't wait to see us either!
  He promised lots of perfect picnic days
  and dancing nights.
  He sends his regards and apologizes for winter.

Cold Breath, Great Lungs

Today is not a sad day
Today is a happy day

Happy days follow happy days
Like great lungs follow cold breath!

A song a day keeps the quiet away.

It's like jazz

That sweet place where I go
It's like jazz, the city life after light rain
A glass of wine and my check, please
Take me like something sovereign in gloves
Across the bricks of the road
To the roar of sparkling lights and flushed faces
Then hide me away in a damp place
Near the water
Kiss me there
and wake up to that memory.

I Love You

It's hard to not
To say I love you to a stranger
A breeze on my back and my blue eyes
They can see
And your brown hair has no knots
Your dance, your hands,
To sing, and you do!
You do sing and you do it well.

Like spring water
A brook from my lungs
Words falling out the door
"I love you" I say in this moment
I'll use the word as if I never knew what love meant.

Certainly I do not love you
But from here
Up here
On my tip toes from enjoyment
From a burst of excitement and awe
Like a grunt from a blow
Out comes "I love you."

Hello to you
Life is a song
I'm not always on pitch
But I'm singing along

Da Capo al Fine

Children dancing is the piano

Wine is the tempo of my company

Fireflies dal niente

And the moon is humming

Picking Stones

My foot moves stones to tone poem tones
As an old man moans of his antique bones.

And it's all getting rusty and covered in dust;
Life, a virgin Shirley, and death is a must.

Eating Cake

"A smirk for myself, please"
Said closing my eyes.
I'm eating cake
And nobody's looking.

I'm having a piece,
But only just one.

I'll thump and I'll bump
Or whisper and squeak.
It's me and my cake,
It's all just for me.

Any taste I can think of,
Any color and cut.
Celebration comes easy
When I'm eating cake.

I am the teacup
I am the piano
Rest me gently
Hold me firmly

i've been rubbing my nose with the face of a storm

my lungs have never felt this good
my eyes have never been so happy

the neighbors lights are throwing fireworks on the ground
fireworks that make the most peaceful sound you'll ever hear

wet concrete
the storm is on the ground

my head is on the ground
i'll lay in bed cuddling with the sound of rain
i'll play with her hair
and she'll lay her hands to rest on me

i will sleep so well
and my dreams will open the doors
to the lightning that reminds me
of what i will see
the very next morning

a very bright life in need of something
a little more than organization

a very bright life that needs actions more than words

Stomach in love
Honey IV
Falling Asleep VI

Bananas on a grapevine and a wooden horse
Lonely in the garden and brides waiting

Sleep is sweet
and water with sugar

Diluted-honey shivers, up the arms
and rain down the neck

Long hair
cute swing set

Bumble bees buzz
Busy busy buildings

Walk on the dock
Atlantic breeze dreams of dreaming daylight hours

Fingers and fingers, more and more
Stomach in love, toes gone cold

I wish my heart was...

That much braver, that much stronger.

I AM WORTH MORE
THAN I THINK

You're not broken, you're just a
Deep Feeling Magic Being.

In the big picture we are all just so very small...

I can't wait to be a part of something big...

All we need is a little hope, life, and magic.

one step at a time
and all for the love

Christmas

Dear Christmas,

You were a girl in snowy eyes
and a woman in humid air.
A small figure making large movements
in more than just the life of a fictional character.
She was a spool of perfection, wrapped to perfection.
She leaked jealousy, love, and compassion.
When she took my heart, she also took my mind.
And we've been placed in separate worlds
And I can see her through my window.
She's so beautiful.

if you're feeling grey
It may be the day
go make some tea
and let it fade away

That feeling of loneliness doesn't go so deep anymore after hearing someone describe it perfectly.

Make every space
A special place

Hold on to the magic that you feel
It will start to slip away

BE SPARKLY,
BE BRIGHT,
BE GLITTER,
AND LIGHT,
ALL DAY,
ALL NIGHT,
BE YOU,
ALRIGHT?

Hope is free.

Tea Tins

There is no way for me, so amateur,
to dance around with words to poetically, politely,
or properly dress the heart of my romantic experience
with every taste of tea I've been so happily a part of.

But I will tell you this —

After a day of riding a Russian Caravan
and diving into a Dragonwell,
I was drying by a Lapsang Souchong
Just to be tempted by Darjeeling
As my Grandfather was talking of a historical Sri Lanka.

And that was it, that's when I realized

Tea
Harmony and strange unity; Complex in taste,
but simple enough for me.

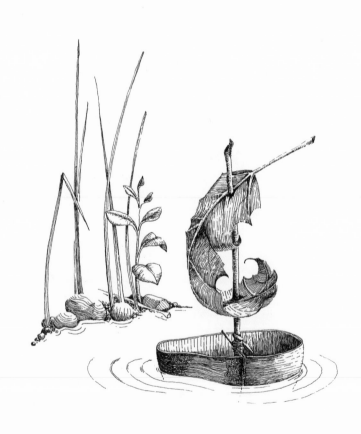

and everything and everything

my mind is liquid

my mind is rubber

i'm bending far and now everything is bending far

i'm kissing my own feet just because i can

you're at a loss for words

i'm out of breath now

i'm curled up like a cat in the sun

here i am resting

as i rest i reach under everything soft to look for new secrets

i get kissed by the people without footsteps

they're my favorite kind of people

there's no sign of them coming and going

they hang upside down and they don't have blood to ruin their mood

i have blood

that's why i'm the cat in the sun

fun jokes now

hot water on my face

nothing else is wet, not the ground

i'm pulled to my feet, but only for a moment

i'm floating now

i'm grey

farewell everyone!

look what i have found!

(The ending was different each time. I caught myself looking
more than once.)

There it was...
And I felt as if it was all I had ever wanted to see.
Alas, the moment ended and I went on,
having lived a better life.

www.secretmidnightpress.com